HOW YOUR BODY WORKS

FUELING THE BODY

DIGESTION AND NUTRITION

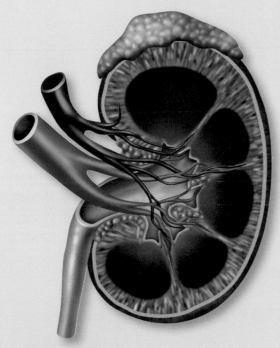

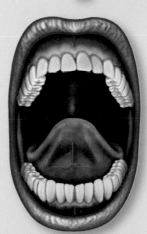

THOMAS CANAVAN

PowerKiDS press™

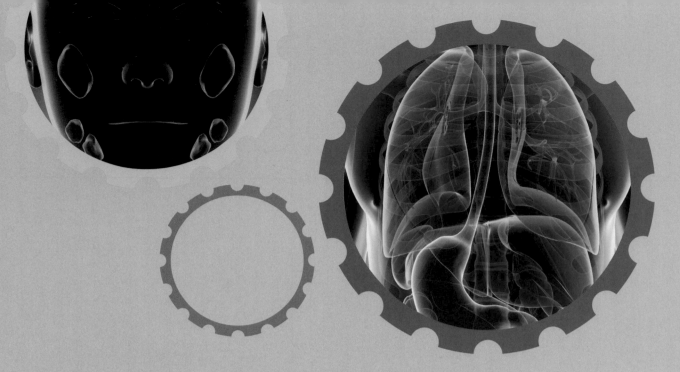

Published in 2016 by
The Rosen Publishing Group, Inc.
29 East 21st Street, New York, NY 10010

Cataloging-in-Publication Data
Canavan, Thomas.
Fueling the body: digestion and nutrition / by Thomas Canavan.
p. cm. — (How your body works)
Includes index.
ISBN 978-1-4994-1227-7 (pbk.)
ISBN 978-1-4994-1251-2 (6 pack)
ISBN 978-1-4994-1239-0 (library binding)
1. Digestion — Juvenile literature. 2. Digestive organs —
Juvenile literature. 3. Gastrointestinal system — Juvenile literature.
I. Canavan, Thomas, 1956-. II. Title.
QP145.C218 2016
612.3—d23

Copyright © 2016 Arcturus Holding Limited

Produced by Arcturus Publishing Limited,

Author: Thomas Canavan
Editors: Joe Harris, Joe Fullman, Nicola Barber and Sam Williams
Designer: Elaine Wilkinson
Original design concept and cover design: Notion Design

Picture Credits: All images courtesy of Shutterstock, apart from:
iStock.com: p9 bottom-right. Science Photo Library: p18 (Dorling
Kindersley). Lee Montgomery and Anne Sharp: back cover, p30, p31.

Manufactured in the United States of America
CPSIA Compliance Information: Batch #WS15PK:
For Further Information contact Rosen Publishing, New York, New York at 1-800-237-9932

CONTENTS

FUELING THE BODY.

Your body has to break down the food you eat in order to get their nutrients, which are the substances you need to keep healthy. This process is called digestion, and it begins the moment food enters your mouth. For your food, this is the start of a long journey. Along the way, your digestive system churns, pushes, squeezes, and breaks down the food until all of the nutrients are released into your body.

The process of digestion usually takes hours, although your body can process some foods and drinks more quickly. Your digestive system has many tools to get the job done efficiently – powerful chemicals, strong acids, expanding organs, and muscles that work continuously without you even realizing it!

OPEN WIDE

Which food do you like best? Is it ice cream or a juicy peach, chips or a delicious pizza? Is your mouth watering even as you think about it? When your mouth starts to produce saliva (or spit) at the idea of something tasty, it's really getting ready to go to work!

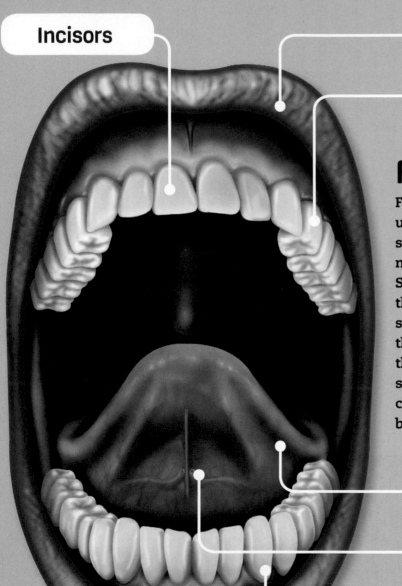

Incisors

Upper lip

Molars

Tongue

Sublingual glands

Canines

Lower lip

FIRST STOP

First, your teeth cut and grind up your food. Depending on their shape and where they are in your mouth, your teeth do different jobs. Sharp, narrow teeth called incisors at the front of your mouth cut food into small bits. The wider molars towards the back of your mouth grind up these pieces of food. Your tongue stands guard, keeping the food close to your teeth until it's been fully chewed.

If you have gelatin for dessert, set a bowl aside. Mix in some pineapple or kiwi and leave for ten minutes. You'll see that the gelatin has become liquid. That's because these fruits contain a chemical that breaks the gelatin down – just as your saliva breaks down the food in your mouth.

JUICY!

Saliva moistens your food and helps to make it mushy. It also helps to break down food that may be trapped between your teeth – so it helps prevent tooth decay as well. A nice smell, such as freshly baked bread, can sometimes "make your mouth water." That's because your senses of smell and taste are very closely linked.

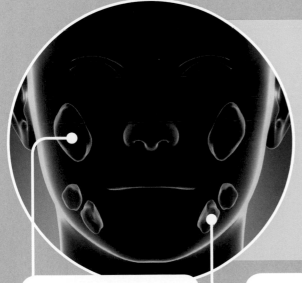

SOAKING IT ALL UP

Saliva is made by glands in your mouth. These are the sublingual glands, which lie below the tongue, and the parotid glands at the back of your mouth. Food needs to be moist before it can be digested. Saliva does that job. It's made of water and other chemicals. One of those chemicals is called amylase, which starts to break down your food even before you swallow.

Parotid glands　　**Sublingual glands**

EASY TO SWALLOW

Once your food has been chewed and softened with saliva, your tongue rolls it into a ball, called a bolus. Then your tongue pushes this mushed-up bolus to the back of your mouth ready for the next stage in your food's digestive journey.

Your mouth contains more bacteria than the combined populations of the United States and Canada.

DOWN THE HATCH

You've chewed that tasty morsel and your tongue has rolled it into a ball. Now it's time to send it on its way to your stomach. But as it heads down your throat, there's a fork in the road: will it go straight to your stomach or wind up stuck in your windpipe?

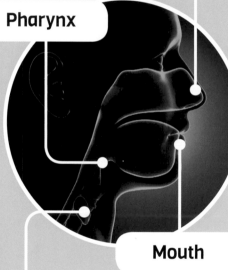

Nose

Pharynx

Mouth

Trachea (windpipe)

SIDE BY SIDE

The pharynx is the area at the back of your mouth that leads into your throat. It deals with both eating and breathing. Your food passes that way, as well as the air being breathed in through your nose. Your food heads down your esophagus, to your stomach. Meanwhile, air passes through your trachea (windpipe) to your lungs. The openings to these two passageways are right next door to each other.

GONE THE WRONG WAY?

If you drink too quickly you may start to cough. That's because some of the liquid went down "the wrong way." When you swallow, a flap called the epiglottis stops liquid and food from entering your trachea. If your epiglottis doesn't close in time, some of the drink may go into your trachea. You automatically cough to send the liquid straight back out, so you don't choke!

SAFE SWALLOWING

You can't eat and breathe at the same time – it would mean keeping both your trachea and esophagus open at the same time. And that would be a recipe for disaster! You'd choke because the food would block your breathing. But a clever bit of design means that just as you are about to swallow, your epiglottis folds down to cover the top of your trachea. So when you swallow, your food heads safely down your esophagus.

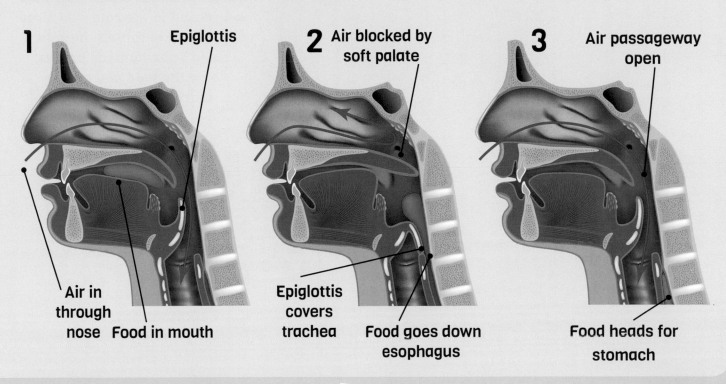

1 Epiglottis

Air in through nose   Food in mouth

2 Air blocked by soft palate

Epiglottis covers trachea   Food goes down esophagus

3 Air passageway open

Food heads for stomach

Burping is the way your body gets rid of air that you accidentally swallowed. In some countries, letting out a soft burp is a sign that you've enjoyed your food!

FEELING THE SQUEEZE

Food doesn't just drop down your esophagus. Circular muscles around your esophagus tighten behind the bolus of food and remain relaxed in front of it. This makes it easier for it to slide down. The process is called peristalsis. It's a bit like eating a frozen ice pop – you squeeze behind the ice to push it out the open end.

STOMACH CHURNING

Your food takes no more than ten seconds to pass through into your stomach. That's where the real process of digestion starts to happen. Your stomach is shaped like a letter J. It is one of the most important organs in your digestive system. A stomach is normally about the size of your fist, but it stretches and gets bigger as you fill it up with food.

GETTING TO WORK

All the work of mashing and churning the food happens in the body of your stomach. This is where those balls of food that come down your esophagus get turned into a mushy liquid. The powerful muscles in the walls of your stomach squeeze the food. At the same time, the stomach wall produces enzymes and strong acids called gastric juices to break down the food further. After some squeezing and dissolving, the food turns into a liquid called chyme.

ACTIVITY

Take an old coin and put it in a glass filled with cola. Leave overnight. The next morning, rinse and remove the coin. It should be much shinier. That's because acid in the cola eats away at the layer of dirt on the coin. Acid in your stomach breaks down the food you eat in much the same way.

Esophagus

Cardiac sphincter

Pylorus sphincter

Pyloric

To small intestine

Powerful muscles

Body of stomach

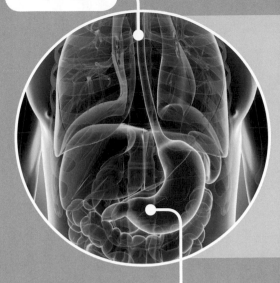

Esophagus

Stomach

ONE-WAY SYSTEM

Your stomach is just one part of a whole series of different organs through which food passes as it's digested. Before entering the stomach, food travels down the esophagus, and after leaving the stomach, it travels into the small intestine at the other end. Special valves called sphincters control the flow of food at each end. They make sure that food travels the right way through your body.

BELLY BALLOON

Your stomach expands just like a balloon as it fills with digested food.

The acid in your stomach is strong enough to dissolve metal – but it wouldn't be a very tasty meal!

BURNING UP

Sometimes, food and gastric juice from the stomach goes the wrong way through a sphincter, back into the gullet. Stomach acid in the base of the esophagus causes heartburn – which can be very painful.

UNDER CONTROL

Special cells in your stomach wall (shown left) allow it to expand. They also control the balance of chemicals – so your stomach doesn't start to digest itself!

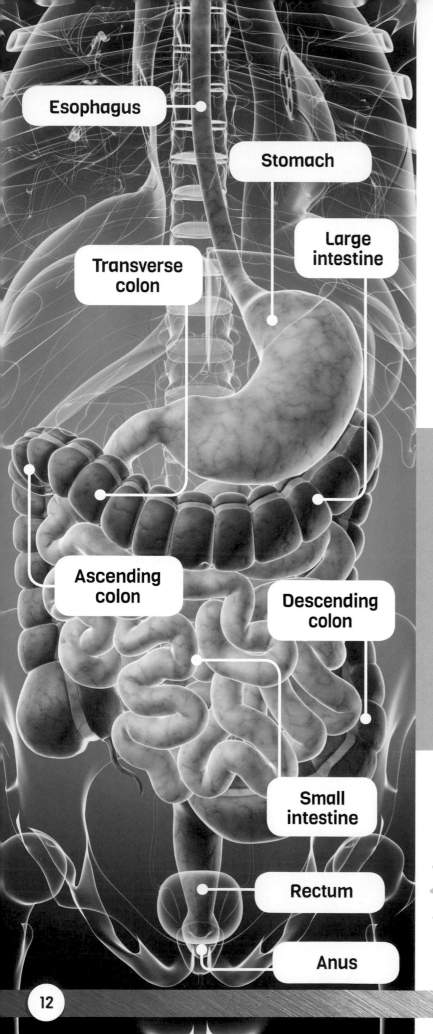

Esophagus

Stomach

Large intestine

Transverse colon

Ascending colon

Descending colon

Small intestine

Rectum

Anus

BIG AND SMALL

All that chewing, mushing, and acid treatment gets your food good and squishy by the time it leaves your stomach. It's now ready for the next stage of digestion – removing the nutrients and getting rid of what's not needed. And this is when the small and large intestines have their starring roles.

NOT SO SMALL!

Your mushed-up food leaves the stomach and enters the small intestine. The small intestine isn't really small – it's just narrower than the large intestine. The food spends around four hours working its way through the sections of this intestine. In the first bit – the duodenum – it gets broken down even further. In the second and third stages, nutrients and vitamins are absorbed into your body's bloodstream.

The small intestine is much longer than the large intestine! Uncoiled, it would stretch 20 feet (6 m). That's more than the height of three basketball players standing on each other's shoulders!

FINGER FOOD

The lining of the small intestine is covered with tiny, narrow shapes called villi (and even tinier microvilli). Through a powerful microscope, villi look like tiny fingers swaying gently as they stir up your food. Villi are very good at removing nutrients and passing them to the blood that's heading to the rest of your body. Some of the villi are only two cells thick – so nutrients can pass through them easily.

LAST CHANCE

The large intestine is your body's last chance to extract nutrients from what you ate hours before. But there's more going on than simply getting the last bits of goodness from the food mixture. Many different types of bacteria live in the large intestine. Some of them produce important vitamins and chemicals. These get absorbed into your bloodstream along with everything else.

EVERY LAST DROP

The large intestine is much shorter than the small intestine, but it's called "large" because it's wider. By the time your food moves into the large intestine, most of the important nutrients have been absorbed, but there's still some more to be collected – along with water. The food mixture (now mostly waste) is pretty dry when it moves through the descending colon into the rectum. And there it stays until you go to the bathroom.

OUT YOU GO!

The rectum is the end of the line as far as your digestive system is concerned. It's like a storage room for waste – waiting there until you go to the bathroom. And when you do, the waste is pushed out through peristalsis, the same way the food was pushed down your esophagus. Sphincter muscles keep your anus – the real end of the line – tightly shut until you decide that you're ready to use the bathroom.

A BALANCED DIET

It's important to eat a healthy, balanced diet to give your body the wide range of nutrients it needs. It's fine to eat pizza or ice cream from time to time – as long as you eat lots of other healthy foods too!

WHAT YOUR BODY NEEDS:

BRAIN – You need magnesium (from leafy vegetables) and vitamin E (present in many nuts) to help the brain to function well.

MUSCLES – Protein (in meat, fish, nuts, and beans) helps build muscles.

BONES – Calcium (in most dairy products) keeps bones strong.

HAIR – Iron, vitamins A and C, protein, and zinc (from a range of foods) keep your hair strong and shiny.

HEART – Your heart is a muscle, so it has all of the requirements of a normal muscle.

SKIN – Vitamin E (in avocados and pine nuts) and the chemicals in many fruits help your skin.

FINGERNAILS – Zinc, protein and some fatty acids (from oily fish) all keep your nails looking good.

IT'S GOOD FOR YOU!

The saying "you are what you eat" is surprisingly true. The minerals, vitamins, and other nutrients in your food are absorbed into your body, becoming part of it. Some help specific parts of your body, such as calcium in milk, which is excellent for building bones and teeth. Others help your whole body. Carbohydrates in pasta and rice give your body energy and keep you moving.

BRAIN FOOD?

For centuries, fish was known as "brain food." Was that just a myth? Scientists now agree that some fatty acids really do help the brain. And the food that contains these acids – actually it's fish!

SUPERFOODS?

Some people describe blueberries, pomegranate juice, garlic, broccoli, and other foods as "superfoods." They claim that these foods and drinks can help fight disease, keep you healthy and even help you live longer. Scientists agree that while all these foods are good for you, they don't work miracles! Far more important is to eat a "super diet" – the balanced diet that gives your body the wide range of nutrients it needs to work well.

NAUGHTY BUT NICE!

Foods such as ice cream and pizza should be occasional treats. Most ice cream contains lots of fat and sugar, and pizza is heavy in fat. Although your body needs some fat in a balanced diet, it doesn't require a lot, and too much of the types of fats found in foods like sausages, cheese, or cookies can cause health problems.

Your body contains enough iron to make a spike large enough to hold your weight!

HELPFUL ALLIES

Many of your body's digestive organs are found close to each other in your abdomen. That's the part of your body that's just above and below your belly button. The liver, pancreas, and gallbladder all play their part in helping you digest food.

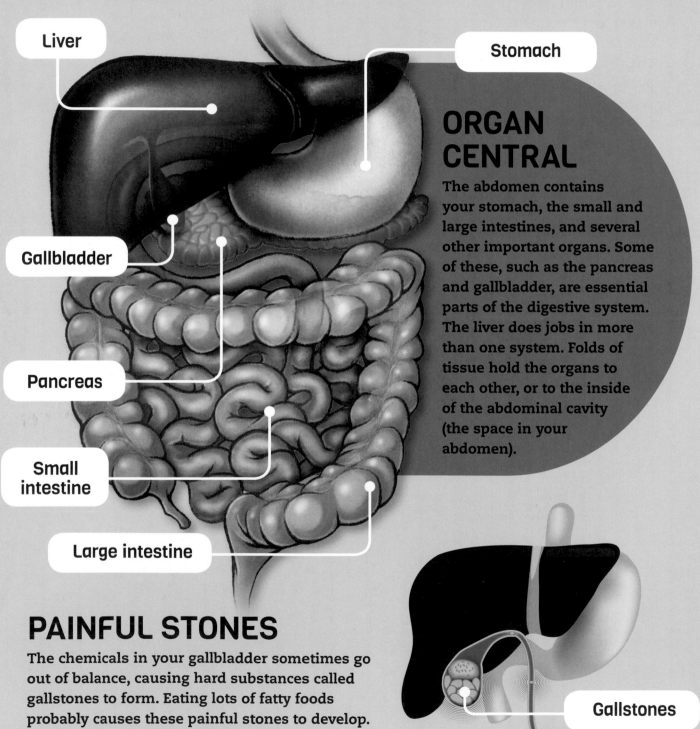

Liver

Stomach

Gallbladder

Pancreas

Small intestine

Large intestine

ORGAN CENTRAL

The abdomen contains your stomach, the small and large intestines, and several other important organs. Some of these, such as the pancreas and gallbladder, are essential parts of the digestive system. The liver does jobs in more than one system. Folds of tissue hold the organs to each other, or to the inside of the abdominal cavity (the space in your abdomen).

PAINFUL STONES

The chemicals in your gallbladder sometimes go out of balance, causing hard substances called gallstones to form. Eating lots of fatty foods probably causes these painful stones to develop.

Gallstones

INTO THE MIX

The pancreas makes substances called enzymes. These are used in your small intestine to break down carbohydrates, proteins, and fats. It also makes and sends a chemical called sodium bicarbonate to the small intestine. The sodium bicarbonate reacts with the acid in the intestine, stopping it from getting too strong and damaging the lining of the small intestine.

ACTIVITY

Sodium bicarbonate is the same as baking soda. Put three teaspoons of baking soda into an empty plastic bottle. Pour in a cup of vinegar and stretch a balloon across the top of the bottle. Soon, the balloon fills up. That's because the baking soda and vinegar (acid) react – just as sodium bicarbonate and acid juices do in the intestine.

STAR PLAYER

If you were asked to name your most important organ, you would probably say your heart (pictured below on the right). But after looking at the liver closely, you might think twice. The liver (shown below on the left) is your largest internal organ. It gives a final check to the blood coming from the digestive system – turning the nutrients into useful substances and filtering out any bad stuff. It also produces bile, a liquid used to break down and digest fat.

LIVER?   #1   HEART?

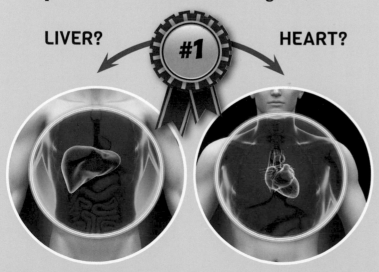

FIGHTING THE FAT

The bile produced by the liver is stored in the gallbladder. You need some fat in your diet because it stores energy for emergencies. So if the food arriving in the small intestine seems a bit fatty, the gallbladder squeezes out some bile. The bile breaks the fat down until it's ready to be absorbed by the body.

BLOOD CLEANING

It's really important for your body to get rid of the waste that it can't use. It sends all the solid waste from food down and out through your rectum. But all the chemical reactions going on in other parts of your body create even more waste. And that waste stays in your blood until it passes through another of your body's amazing systems – your kidneys.

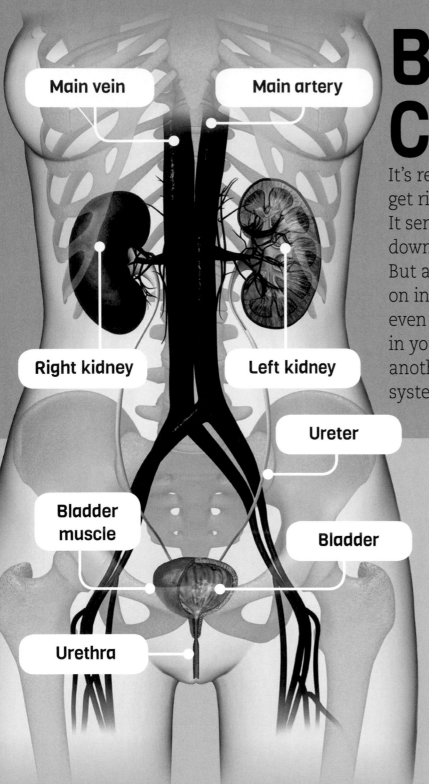

Main vein

Main artery

Right kidney

Left kidney

Ureter

Bladder muscle

Bladder

Urethra

CLEANING SYSTEM

Your body always has about 1.3 gallons (5 l) of blood flowing through it. The blood that leaves the digestive system is full of nutrients that are processed in other parts of the body. The chemical reactions that have processed the nutrients leave waste behind. So as the blood makes its way back to your heart, it passes through your two kidneys so it can be cleaned.

WATER WORKS

The kidneys filter your blood and the waste goes into a liquid, which is mostly water. This is called urine. The second part of the kidneys' job is to get rid of the urine, so the wastes don't remain in your body.

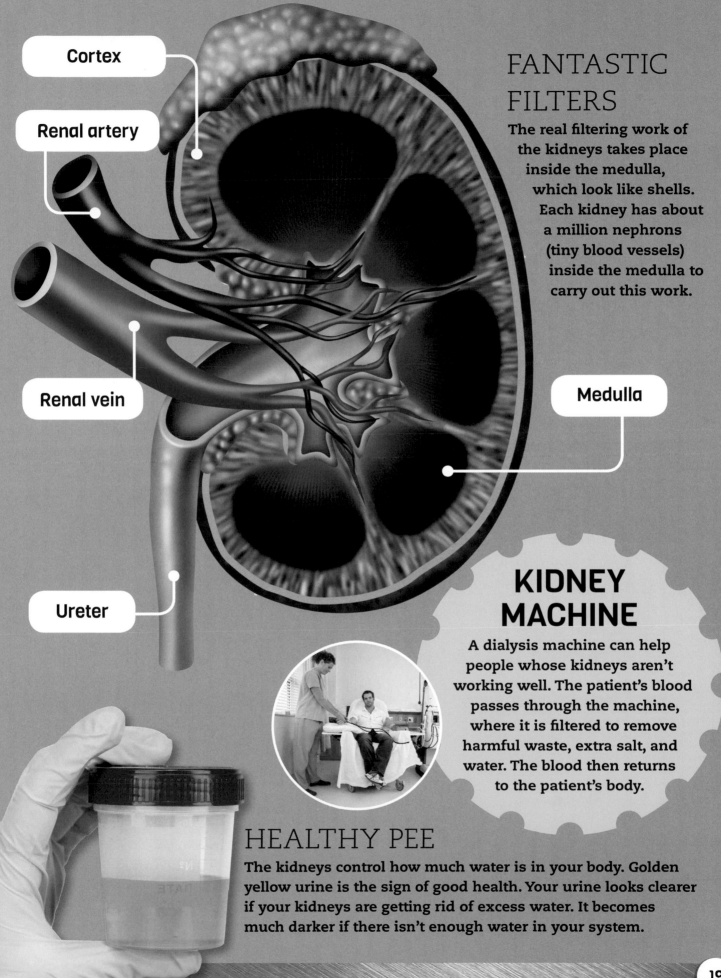

Cortex

Renal artery

Renal vein

Ureter

Medulla

FANTASTIC FILTERS

The real filtering work of the kidneys takes place inside the medulla, which look like shells. Each kidney has about a million nephrons (tiny blood vessels) inside the medulla to carry out this work.

KIDNEY MACHINE

A dialysis machine can help people whose kidneys aren't working well. The patient's blood passes through the machine, where it is filtered to remove harmful waste, extra salt, and water. The blood then returns to the patient's body.

HEALTHY PEE

The kidneys control how much water is in your body. Golden yellow urine is the sign of good health. Your urine looks clearer if your kidneys are getting rid of excess water. It becomes much darker if there isn't enough water in your system.

THE BIG THREE

CARBOHYDRATES
These break down into sugars that give you quick energy.

PROTEINS
The strength in your muscles is thanks to proteins.

FATS
These provide a "storehouse" for energy.

THE POWER STATION

The digestive system – working all the way from your teeth to your stomach and intestines – does a great job of extracting all the nutrients that your body needs. You've also done your bit by making sure that your diet includes a good balance of carbohydrates, proteins and fats. So what happens to those nutrients once they've been sent off from the intestines?

GOOD NUTRITION

Your body needs a wide range of nutrients. The "big three" group of nutrients are carbohydrates, proteins and fats. Some foods contain lots of one group. For example, a steak is high in protein and butter has lots of fat. But your overall diet should be a balance between them. A chicken sandwich is a good example of food that provides some of all three: the bread has carbohydrates, the chicken supplies protein and the avocado supplies the fat.

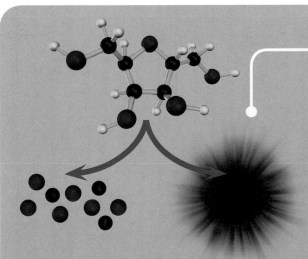

During a match, tennis players often eat bananas. They are easy to digest and are high in carbohydrates, which the body uses to produce energy.

POWER UP

Proteins in food are broken down into pieces called amino acids. Your body then puts the amino acids back together to make different proteins that carry out special jobs. These new proteins help other chemical reactions, allow cells to communicate with each other, and even provide energy if there isn't enough carbohydrate or fat.

BREAKING THINGS DOWN

To release energy and keep you moving, your body uses chemical reactions to break down carbohydrates and fats. The bonds that hold some molecules together contain lots of energy, and breaking them apart releases that energy. This breaking down of bonds is called the catabolic process.

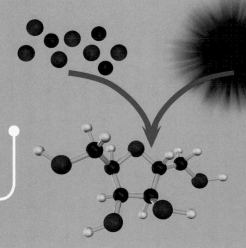

BUILDING THINGS UP

The opposite of the catabolic process is the anabolic process. Your body works with smaller molecules to produce larger ones. In this way it also builds new proteins.

AN ACTIVE YOU!

Together with a good, balanced diet, exercise helps to keep your body running smoothly. Getting some exercise, such as playing a sport or going to a gym, also helps you to stay at a healthy weight.

Lungs
Breathing deeply helps the lungs stay strong

Muscles
Regular exercise strengthens muscles

Waistline
Energy needed for exercise burns some of the fat stored around your waist

Joints
Exercise keeps joints moving well

During your lifetime, you will eat about 60,000 pounds (27,000 kg) of food – about the weight of six elephants!

BURNING CALORIES

A "calorie" is a unit used to measure the energy stored in food and in your body. When you eat, the calories in food are turned into energy. If you eat more calories than your body needs for energy, those extra calories get stored as fat. Your body uses up calories just breathing, moving, and thinking! But when you exercise, you need more energy, so your body burns up some of the calories stored as fat.

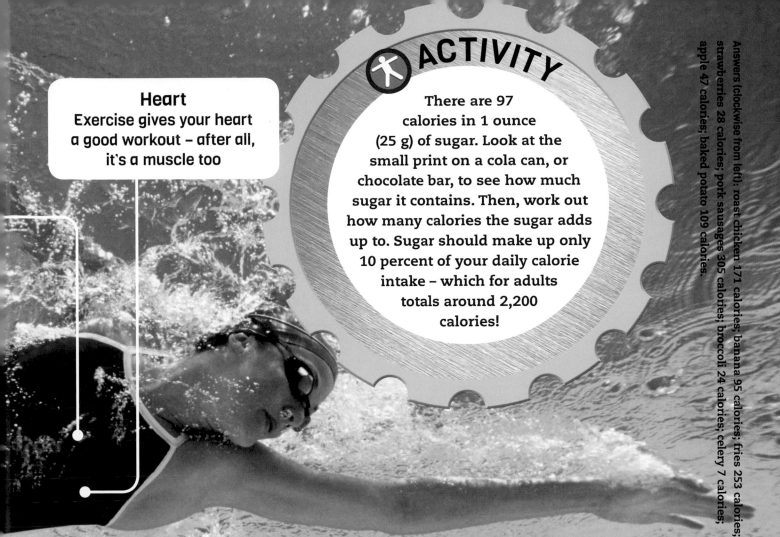

Heart
Exercise gives your heart a good workout – after all, it's a muscle too

✦ ACTIVITY

There are 97 calories in 1 ounce (25 g) of sugar. Look at the small print on a cola can, or chocolate bar, to see how much sugar it contains. Then, work out how many calories the sugar adds up to. Sugar should make up only 10 percent of your daily calorie intake – which for adults totals around 2,200 calories!

Answers (clockwise from left): roast chicken 171 calories; banana 95 calories; fries 253 calories; strawberries 28 calories; pork sausages 305 calories; broccoli 24 calories; celery 7 calories; apple 47 calories; baked potato 109 calories.

HOW MANY CALORIES?
There are 95 calories in 4 oz (100 g) of banana. Guess how many calories there are in 4 oz (100 g) of these foods. Answers are on the right.

Pork sausages

Banana

Fries

Broccoli

Strawberries

Apple

Roast chicken   Baked potato

Celery

DID YOU KNOW?

WHEN YOU BLUSH THE LINING OF YOUR STOMACH ALSO BLUSHES

Your body produces a hormone called adrenaline when it needs to deal with stress. The adrenaline makes blood vessels widen so that more blood can flow through them. This increased flow causes certain areas of your body that contain lots of blood vessels – like your cheeks and stomach lining – to redden.

A TRADITIONAL DIET OF MEAT AND FISH KEEPS INUIT PEOPLE FREE OF MANY DISEASES

The Inuit people of the Arctic regions in the far north traditionally had little chance to eat fruit, vegetables, or grains – foods that are considered essential for a balanced diet. In fact, the same vitamins and nutrients are plentiful in the types of oils and fats found in Arctic fish and meat.

AN ADULT WOULD HAVE TO RUN FOR 50 MINUTES TO BURN OFF THE CALORIES IN A SINGLE CAN OF COLA

Calories are a measure of energy. If you eat or drink more calories than you burn off through exercise, then you gain weight. You lose weight if you either eat less or exercise more. So an adult would need to exercise hard for nearly an hour to burn off the amount of energy – counted in calories – in one cola.

SALIVA
HAS LOTS OF DIFFERENT JOBS

Your salivary glands produce up to 53 fluid ounces (1.5 l) of this slippery liquid every day. And although the main job of saliva is to help begin the process of digestion, it performs other roles even when you're not eating. Saliva keeps your mouth moist, allowing you to swallow and speak, and it also helps to protect your teeth from harmful bacteria.

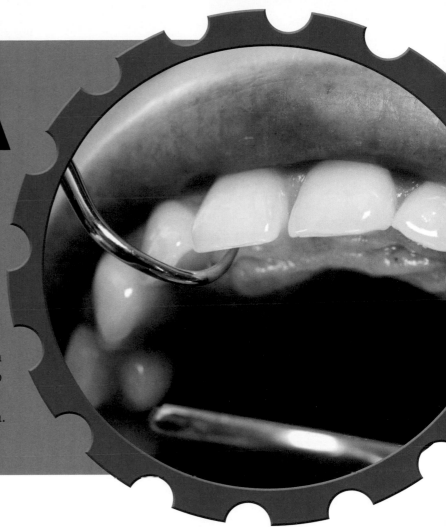

OPENING
YOUR MOUTH
TO EAT DOESN'T JUST LET THE
THE FOOD IN

As you open your mouth the air that flows in either raises or lowers the temperature of the food, to help it match your body temperature. Lots of what goes on when you digest food could be described as chemical reactions. And temperature plays a big part in making sure these reactions work. If one ingredient – such as very hot food or a very cold drink – is at the wrong temperature, then your digestive enzymes and acids can't work as well.

DOES CHEWING GUM

STAY INSIDE YOU FOR YEARS?

It's never a good idea to swallow gum – but the quick answer is no, gum doesn't stay inside for years. Chewing gum has four main ingredients – chemicals to give it taste, softeners, sweeteners, and the gum base. Your body can digest the first three easily. The gum base is added so that you can chew it without digesting it. If you do swallow the gum, your digestive system recognizes it and passes it out like any other waste. But if you swallow too much gum at one time things could become blocked up and painful for a while "down below."

CAN YOU STILL SWALLOW AND DIGEST FOOD EVEN IF YOU ARE UPSIDE-DOWN?

Yes. And it's easy to understand why if you think of food traveling to your stomach from your mouth rather than down to your stomach. Your body doesn't need gravity to move the food along. Muscles in your esophagus push the food along. As the food is pushed, the muscles behind it tighten and block it from going back to your mouth – even if you're upside-down.

WHAT MAKES YOUR STOMACH RUMBLE?

It rumbles because it's doing its job, except a little ahead of time! Your brain sends a signal to your digestive system when it senses food is on the way – maybe after you've bought a lovely cold ice cream or smelled some delicious pizza in the oven. The signals starts the muscles in your stomach and intestines tightening and loosening, just as they do when there's food to digest. But because they're empty, and there's no food to absorb the sounds, you hear rumbling.

IS IT SAFE TO EXERCISE AFTER YOU'VE EATEN?

It can be, but doctors warn people not to exercise on a full – or an empty – stomach. Your digestive system needs blood to do its job, and it needs more blood after a big meal. The muscles you use to exercise also need blood, so you should be careful if you exercise hard after eating: you won't perform as well and you might get stomach cramps. But you shouldn't "run on empty" either: those exercising muscles need the nutrients that are released by digestion. So make sure you eat before you exercise, but leave some time between the two.

SYSTEMS OF THE BODY

Skeletal system

The skeletal system supports and protects your body.

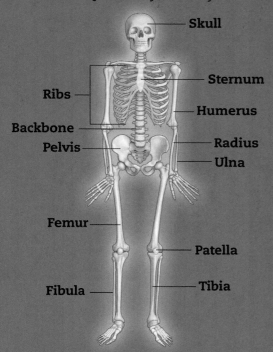

- Skull
- Sternum
- Ribs
- Humerus
- Backbone
- Pelvis
- Radius
- Ulna
- Femur
- Patella
- Fibula
- Tibia

Muscular system

The muscular system moves your body.

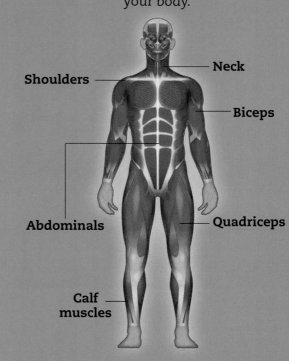

- Neck
- Shoulders
- Biceps
- Abdominals
- Quadriceps
- Calf muscles

Circulatory system

The circulatory system moves blood around your body.

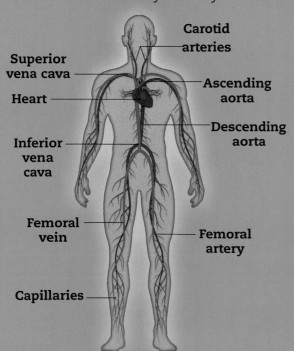

- Carotid arteries
- Superior vena cava
- Ascending aorta
- Heart
- Descending aorta
- Inferior vena cava
- Femoral vein
- Femoral artery
- Capillaries

Respiratory system

The respiratory system controls your breathing.

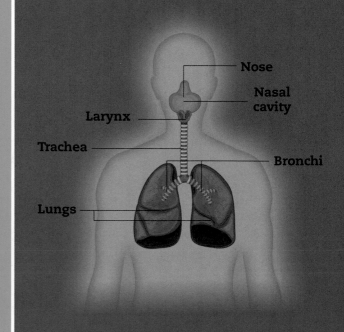

- Nose
- Nasal cavity
- Larynx
- Trachea
- Bronchi
- Lungs

This is your quick reference guide to the main systems of the body: skeletal, muscular, respiratory, circulatory, digestive, nervous, endocrine, and lymphatic.

Digestive system

The digestive system takes food in and out of your body.

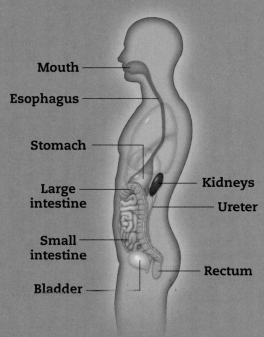

Mouth
Esophagus
Stomach
Large intestine
Kidneys
Ureter
Small intestine
Rectum
Bladder

Nervous system

The nervous system carries messages around your body and controls everything you do.

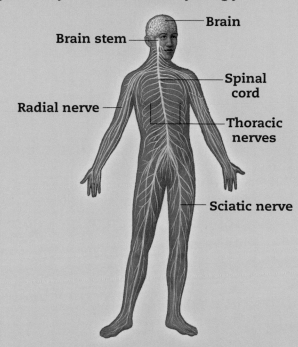

Brain
Brain stem
Spinal cord
Radial nerve
Thoracic nerves
Sciatic nerve

Endocrine system

The endocrine system produces hormones and controls your growth and mood.

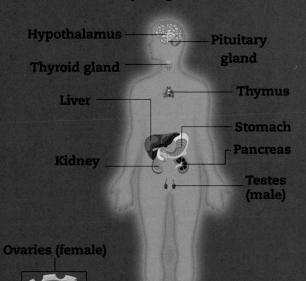

Hypothalamus
Pituitary gland
Thyroid gland
Thymus
Liver
Stomach
Pancreas
Kidney
Testes (male)
Ovaries (female)

Lymphatic system

The lymphatic system fights off germs and helps keep your body healthy.

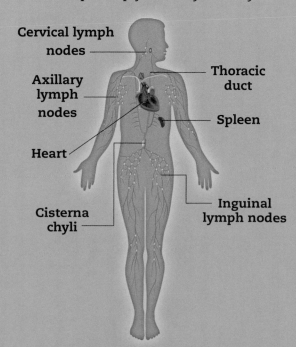

Cervical lymph nodes
Thoracic duct
Axillary lymph nodes
Spleen
Heart
Inguinal lymph nodes
Cisterna chyli

GLOSSARY

abdomen The area of your body just above and below your belly button. It contains your stomach, intestines, and several other major organs.

amino acid An essential nutrient containing several chemical elements.

bacteria Tiny one-celled organisms.

bile A yellowish-brown fluid produced by the liver, stored in the gallbladder, which helps to break down fat.

calcium A chemical that is essential in the body for healthy bones and teeth.

calorie A unit for measuring the energy contained in food.

carbohydrate A type of sugar made by plants that the body uses to produce and store energy.

digestion The breakdown of food into substances that can be easily absorbed into the bloodstream.

enzyme A special protein that helps chemical reactions occur.

epiglottis The flap that folds down to prevent food going down the trachea.

esophagus The foodpipe that connects the throat and the stomach.

fat A chemical substance that the body produces to store energy. It is stored in fat cells beneath the skin or surrounding organs.

gland An organ that regulates the release of hormones into the bloodstream.

hormone A chemical that helps to regulate processes such as reproduction and growth.

incisors The sharp teeth at the front of the mouth used to cut food into small pieces.

intestines The large and small intestines are the part of the digestive system where nutrients are released from the food into the bloodstream.

kidneys The organs that filter waste products from the blood.

liver A major organ in the digestive system which has many jobs including filtering the blood coming from the digestive system.

mineral A chemical substance, such as iron, which is important for health but which the body cannot produce.